TO: JEFF,
BEST WISHES!

'99

Gee Bee

Delmar Benjamin and Steve Wolf

MBI Publishing Company

Dedication

This book is dedicated to Zantford Granville and Pete Miller, without whose creative spirit and enduring labors the building of this Gee Bee replica would have remained a dream.

First published in 1993 by MBI Publishing Company, PO Box 1, 729 Prospect Avenue, Osceola, WI 54020-0001 USA

The information in this book is true and complete to the best of our knowledge. All recommendations are made without any guarantee on the part of the author or Publisher, who also disclaim any liability incurred in connection with the use of this data or specific details.

We recognize that some words, model names, and designations, for example, mentioned herein are the property of the trademark holder. We use them for identification purposes only. This is not an official publication.

MBI Publishing Company books are also available at discounts in bulk quantity for industrial or sales-promotional use. For details write to Special Sales Manager at Motorbooks International Wholesalers & Distributors, 729 Prospect Avenue, PO Box 1, Osceola, WI 54020-0001 USA.

Library of Congress Cataloging-in-Publication Data
Benjamin, Delmar
  Gee bee / Delmar Benjamin, Steve Wolf.
    p. cm. — (Enthusiast color series)
  Includes index.
  ISBN 0-87938-820-X
  1. Gee-Bee (Racing plane)—History. 2. Granville Airplane Company. I. Wolf, Steve. II. Title. III. Series.
TL685.6.B46   1993
629.133'343—dc20   93-13065

On the front cover: Probably one of the best known shapes in aviation, the Gee Bee R-2. The original R-2 was renowned both for its tricky handling and air race successes. *EAA/Jim Koepnick*

On the frontispiece: The Gee Bee doesn't become a flying machine until it reaches 120 mph—over twice the speed at which most airplanes become airborne. *Ray Conkling*

On the title page: The Gee Bee R-2 replica taxiing for takeoff. *Shirley Maule*

On the back cover: Knife-edge flight—what the Gee Bee does best. Oregon's *South Sister Mountain* is in the background. *Ray Conkling*

Printed in Hong Kong

Contents

Acknowledgments

Thanks to: our wives, Tana Benjamin and Liz Wolf, who helped so much in the construction and promotion of this airplane; the people that donated materials to the project: Dave Anderson, Kevin Batterton, Ron Coleman, Frank Gurko, Jim Jenkins, Holly Robinson, Norm Taylor, Sam Thompson, and others; those who donated drawings: Vern Clements, Scott Crosby, Premo Gelletti, Tom Johnson, David Lednicer, Rudy Profant, Walt Redfern, and others; the people that labored on the R-2 and gave their support: Herb Andersen, Keith Antcliff, James Beranek, Anne Byers, Ron Copeland, Lee Dubay, Ed and Pearl Granville, Bill Harsey, Charlie Knight, Marty Landeen, James McAllister, Robert North, Curtis Pitts, Ted Robinson, Jack Rose, Duane Trappen, Mike Yeager, Jim Younkin, and many more; those that donated photos: Maureen and Vern Clements, Ray Conkling, Tom Chrowder, Henry Haffke, Shirley Maule, Doc Nichol, Russ Peltzer, Max Schultz, Dave Schwartz, Bob and Judy Staley, Gary Thompson, Jay Tollbert, Rafe Tomsett, and others; and, finally, to all the Gee Bee fans that have given all manner of support. Without you, the Gee Bee is history.

Foreword

By Pete Miller

Congratulations to you, Steve Wolf and Delmar Benjamin, for your ingenuity in building and flying the Gee Bee R-2 replica. It is a beautiful airplane—so perfectly built and perfectly flown. It seems to me that you have made a forward gain in aviation.

Howell "Pete" Miller

Introduction

In the history of aviation, the period from the late 1920s to the mid-1930s was known as "The Golden Age of Air Racing." Aviation pioneers from the military, aircraft companies, as well as lone individuals strove for speed. Air races offered thousands of dollars in prize money during the money-tight Great Depression, hence aircraft builders were enticed to produce race planes. Little did they know that in just a few short years their aircraft design efforts would be put to use in World War II. Some of the top race plane designers and pilots such as Tony LeVie, Bob Hall, Jimmy Doolittle, Howell W. "Pete" Miller and many others went on to build and fly the fighters and bombers that made victory possible.

The Granville brothers of Springfield, Massachusetts, built some of the most famous race planes of this time. Known as the Gee Bees, their airplanes won many races and set new Shell Speed Dash records. Their racing aircraft made use of new and bold design con-cepts to squeeze as much speed out of the powerplants as possible. In 1931, the Gee Bee Model Z won the Thompson Trophy race in Cleveland, Ohio, showing the world that the Granville Brothers could build the fastest air-planes in America. That same year, during a speed dash attempt, the Model Z shed a wing and rolled into the ground, killing pilot Low-ell Bayles. This was the beginning of a run of bad luck that would plague the Granville's rac-ing aircraft.

With the 1932 races just a half year away, Granville Brothers Aircraft hired a new engi-neer, Howell W. "Pete" Miller, a performance specialist fresh out of school and brimming with innovative ideas. Led by the elder

Opposite page
The Gee Bee R-2 has become the icon of air racing. Even people not familiar with aviation and airplanes recognize the little Golden Age racer. *EAA/Jim Koepnick*

The shape of the R-model Gee Bees has fired the imagination of armchair racers and engineers for six decades. It has also intimidated a good many pilots. *Ray Conkling*

Granville brother, Zantford "Granny" Granville, the four brothers and Miller set out to build two new planes for the upcoming races. The racers would be designated the Model R-1 and R-2 and powered by engines on loan from Pratt & Whitney. The R-1 was designed and built around the new R-1340ci nine-cylinder, supercharged engine which produced 800hp. Built for the Thompson Trophy race, a pylon course, it would be a short-range airplane for all-out speed. The R-2, on the

other hand, was built for the Bendix Trophy race, where long-range and speed were needed. Consequently, the R-2 was powered by the R-985ci Pratt & Whitney engine developing 535hp. Burning less fuel than its bigger brother, the R-2 could fly the race with fewer stops, giving it a better overall speed. The main difference between the two airplanes, other than engines, was that the R-2 held 302gal of fuel versus the 160gal of the R-1. There were other slight differences as well, such as the shapes of the vertical fin and rudder, and the R-2's fixed tailwheel versus the R-1's steerable tailwheel.

In the hands of Jimmy Doolittle, the R-1 won the 1932 Thompson Trophy race. At that time Doolittle also set a new world landplane speed record of 296mph in the Shell Speed Dash, a straight line course. Lee Gehlbach, flying the R-2, finished fourth in the Bendix due to oil leak problems and fifth in the Thompson. Once again, the Granville Brothers brought home the trophies. They were on top of the world. Then in 1933, in the hands of pilot Russell Thaw, the R-2 stalled on landing approach at Indianapolis, rolled, and hit the wingtip. Although he recovered with only wing and landing gear damage, the R-2 was out of the race. Russ Boardman, pilot of the R-1, was shaken by Thaw's accident and, pulling the R-1 off prematurely, stalled and caught a wingtip, flipping the plane onto its back. Boardman died from the injuries.

The R-2 was repaired and while landing at Springfield in 1933, James Haizlip found himself floating too far down the 2,000ft runway. As was done with most airplanes of that period, he kicked the rudder to sideslip and kill the speed. This caused one wing to stall, and once again the R-2 found itself rolled into a ball. Haizlip escaped without serious injuries, barring his pride.

Granville Brothers Aircraft used parts from both crashed airplanes to build the R-1/R-2, a hybrid model initially flown by Roy Minor. During a test flight out of Springfield, he made thirteen landing attempts before finally getting it on the deck; whereupon he slid off the end of the runway with the brakes locked. The airplane caught its wheels in a ditch, performed a complete somersault, and landed upright on the road.

After another trip through the shop, the R-1/R-2 ended up with Cecil Allen. Despite warnings from Miller and Granville, Allen installed a large fuel tank well aft of the center of gravity (cg). The two designers feared the cg would be moved so far back that the plane would be impossible to fly. Ignoring their warnings, Allen took off with the tank full, lost control, crashed, and was killed. Thus ended the R-1 and R-2 racers. They would not be rebuilt.

Until now.

This is the story of how and why we—Delmar Benjamin and Steve Wolf—came to build and fly a Gee Bee replica. We hope we can give you a sense of how we felt and what we gained from the research, building, test flights, air shows, and the smiles and tears of the people associated with this spectacular little airplane. Steve Wolf tells the story of the plane's construction and its first flight (chapters 1–3), then Delmar Benjamin provides some firsthand insight into the flying characteristics of the Gee Bee R-2 (chapters 4–6).

Co-author and airplane builder Steve Wolf, owner of Wolf Aircraft. *Dave Weiman*

Co-author and R-2 owner/pilot Delmar Benjamin. *EAA/Bob Miller*

Chapter 1

Dream to Reality

An early winter descended on the Black Hills of South Dakota during the fall of 1983, forcing the Northern Knights aerobatic team to put down. While waiting out the storm in a Rapid City motel room, Knights team member Delmar Benjamin and I discussed the different types of airplanes we would like to fly. I can remember Delmar saying, "If there was a Gee Bee on the ramp, I'd fly it." Being an air show pilot myself, I had to agree.

However, it wasn't until the spring of 1989, when Delmar sold his Bucker Jungmann—"I'm tired of traveling two miles a minute," he explained—that we started talking about actually building a Gee Bee. We joked about how it might fly. Maybe we would each fly it once and it would scare us so bad that we would donate it to a museum. Then again, maybe it really was a flyable airplane. The fact that this airplane could fly to and from air shows at four miles per minute

particularly appealed to us. In the beginning we talked of building this airplane as a joint venture. Having both flown show planes in air shows, we felt the demand for a Gee Bee would allow one or the other of us to fly it at shows. Our goal was to fly the plane at least 100 hours. If we could accomplish this, then we could dispel some of the Gee Bee myths.

Of the many models built by the Granville Brothers Aircraft Company, we needed to choose one. This was easy. The most famous combination of race plane and pilot was Jimmy Doolittle and the big, red and white R-1 number 11 Thompson Trophy racer. However, we knew that we would be working on a budget and that the airplane had to be capable of making it to the next airport. An engine failure and forced landing would be catastrophic. We

Opposite page
Benjamin warms up the R-2 replica prior to flight.
L.L. Coombs

spoke with Tulsa Aircraft Engines, and they felt the R-985 Pratt & Whitney the Granvilles had used in the R-2 had a slightly better reliability record than the R-1340 used in the R-1. In addition, it was a lighter (about 180lb) and more economical engine. A lighter engine would lower the empty weight and thus decrease wing loading. Considering the fact that Lee Gehlbach had flown the original R-2 some thirty-one hours, including the Bendix Trophy race, without damaging it or himself, the Gee Bee R-2 became our choice.

The time had come to get serious and develop a project plan. It was decided that I would build the welded framework and the main woodwork and perform final assembly at my aircraft shop (Wolf Aircraft) in Oregon. Delmar, who lives on a farm in Montana, would do the metal pounding. The Gee Bee would be test flown out of my shop.

Back to 1932

Other than a few books and magazine articles that we had collected over the years, we had little research material. A call to Walt Redfern, famous for his beautiful World War I replicas, ultimately brought us drawings of the Granville Brothers' airplanes via the Smithsonian National Air and Space Museum. Although most of the drawings were of E and

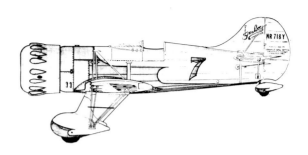

Y Model

Y models, experience has taught me that most designers and builders develop a style that tends to follow through all the airplanes they build. Since the R Model's layout was very similar to the E's, it was clear these drawings might help.

I also learned that the original R-1 drawings, some 300 sheets, were still in existence and had been redrawn by Tom Tumicki of the Connecticut Aeronautical Historical Society. This was very exciting news; original drawings would make building an accurate replica a breeze.

When I called Tumicki, however, I learned that the Granville family wished that the drawings not be reproduced. They were concerned that if an operable airplane was built and flown it would likely crash, further tarnishing the Granville reputation. Delmar and I looked at it in quite the opposite way: If a flying airplane was built and flown successfully, it would prove the Gee Bee was a good airplane.

Left
Delmar Benjamin's keen flying ability is evident here as he flies his Bucker Jungmann inverted. The tail is less than 4ft above the ground!
Delmar Benjamin

T hose short, stubby planes [Gee Bees] were all wrong from a standpoint of longitudinal and directional stability and torque control. Any simple aeronautic textbook would have condemned them from the first page. They were literally accidents looking for a place to happen.

—Roger Huntington,
Thompson Trophy Racers

Our luck started to improve. A new book, *Gee Bee, The Real Story of the Granville Brothers and Their Marvelous Airplanes,* by Henry A. Haffke, had just appeared on the market. A call to Haffke—a noted Gee Bee historian—brought more information. He told us that the New England Air Museum (NEAM) at Windsorlocks, Connecticut, was building an exact, nonflying replica of the R-1 using the original drawings. He also informed us that Pete Miller, the R-Model airplanes' chief engineer, lived near the museum.

A trip to the NEAM in November 1989 proved to be both interesting and rewarding.

We met with the head of the R-1 replica project, Bob North, and told him of our plans to build a flying Gee Bee R-2. This really put him on the spot. The museum had the drawings on loan with the understanding that they would not be used to build a flying airplane. Now we appeared asking for access to their replica to take photographs and make our own sketches. North had no idea who we were, whether we were really capable of such an endeavor, and if letting us have information based on their replica was the same as letting us use the protected drawings. However, I got the feeling that North wanted to see a Gee Bee fly in his lifetime, and I think that our insistence that we were going to build one finally overcame his initial hesitation.

The museum was in the process of plywood-skinning a wing panel on its beautiful replica. At first glance, this airplane is stunning. Photographs don't prepare you for its size. It's big in diameter at 61in, yet it's small at just 17ft long. My impression was a cross between a P-47 Thunderbolt and a Pitts Special. The day was spent taking photographs, recording information, and constructing mental pictures of how the Granvilles built the airplane.

We then headed to the beautiful mountains of Vermont, where Henry Haffke owns and operates an inn. Haffke enthusiastically showed us his one-quarter scale R-1 model. We knew our airplane would be flyable when he told us that his model would fly knife-edge (wings vertical to the horizon as the plane flies a straight line) with very little or no top rudder.

Steve Wolf studying the horizontal stabilizer jack screw of NEAM's R-1 replica. Raising and lowering the rear spar changes the angle of incidence, thus trimming the airplane. *Delmar Benjamin*

The next stop was a meeting with R-model engineer Pete Miller, the man that had designed, wind-tunnel tested, and calculated the performance of the most famous racers ever built. In the days before computers, Miller used a slide rule to determine that the

I knew in the back of my mind, with Delmar at the controls, this airplane would be flown inverted.

—Steve Wolf

R-1 would top out at 298mph. It did 296.2mph with Doolittle at the controls. He told us that of the eleven airplanes for which he had calculated top speed he was always within 5mph.

Miller showed us the 1931 aeronautical engineering manual he used to design the R-Model Gee Bees. He recalled things about the Gee Bees with incredible detail and sketched out cowl pressures and wing wire attachments for us from memory. We left Miller feeling really good about building the R-2. Maybe we could dispel some of the myths surrounding the Gee Bee.

On the long trip home, I couldn't help but think of Miller and his life after the Gee Bees were gone. I was sure that all the stories and books written on the Gee Bees through the years had to bother him. Was the reputation of the airplane really justified? Or was it just so far ahead of its time that the airports and pilots weren't ready? If Jimmy Doolittle and Lee Gehlbach, both experienced test pilots, could fly Gee Bees successfully, then could it really be a good airplane with a good pilot? Both Doolittle and Gehlbach described it as a flyable, though unstable, airplane but said that as long as you flew it constantly, it was alright. After meeting Miller, I just couldn't help feeling that the truth needed to be known.

Another break in the project came when a complete set of drawings and the fuselage lay-out formula were donated by Vern Clements, a Gee Bee fanatic who has built extremely accurate flying models based on his own Miller-verified drawings. After hundreds of late night hours, I had the construction drawings to a point where we could start the project. All that remained was to figure out any changes that would be required.

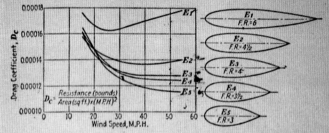

Streamline Shapes. An almost unlimited variety of shapes of streamline form have been tested, and a number have been found which offer a very low resistance to airflow. The proportions and drag characteristics of a series of five geometrically similar shapes of good streamline form are shown in Fig. 9. The effects of wind speed and fineness ratio are evident. A number of other

FIG. 9.—Proportions and drag characteristics of a series of geometrically similar stream line shapes. (*British Advisory Committee, R. & M.*, 311.)

representative streamline shapes and their resistance properties are indicated in Fig. 10. The drag coefficients stated are in all cases those corresponding to the highest Reynolds number at which tests were conducted.

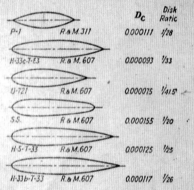

FIG. 10.—Representative streamline bodies and their resistance coefficients. (Note: Disk ratio is the relation of the resistance of the body to that of a flat disk of equal cross-sectional area.)

In practical design it is seldom possible to attain the low resistance values of pure streamline shapes. Modifications in shape must be made, and many accessories and attachments must be added which break up the smooth flow of air around the body, and which usually multiply the resistance many times. The high resistance of the best fuselage designs, as compared with the resist-

Left
Hundreds of reference photographs were taken of the under-construction R-1 replica at the New England Air Museum. Although it's being built based on the original drawings, it's for static display only and will never fly. *Delmar Benjamin*

Engineer Pete Miller's 1931 aeronautical engineering book shows that the least drag is a teardrop shape with a length three times the diameter. The widest point is one-third of the way back. The Gee Bee's large-diameter fuselage is the embodiment of this formula. *Delmar Benjamin*

Chapter 2

Changes for the 1990s

Free advice, it is said, is worth what you pay for it, and on this project we received plenty of it. Most of it concerned ways in which we should try to improve the Gee Bee's flying qualities. No matter how hard we tried to explain that the finished airplane wouldn't be a Gee Bee if we made any changes in its aerodynamic design, people just didn't understand. How would we really know how an R-2 flew if we increased the wing area or used a full-thick M-6 airfoil? Or if we added length to the fuselage or more vertical fin? Changing anything to enhance the flying qualities would not prove that the Granville brothers had just suffered bad luck. Miller would know in his heart that people would be saying, "Of course Delmar's Gee Bee hasn't crashed, they made it more stable by adding two feet to the fuselage."

Today pilots typically fly off big, long, paved runways. In the 1930s they flew off grass, which allowed airplanes to use tail skids or tailwheels locked straight. Most airplanes had no brakes, or brakes that weren't very good. The R-2 was no exception. It had mechanically operated shoe brakes that were connected both to the control stick, and the heels of the rudder pedals. To get braking action you pushed with your heels and pulled back on the stick for more pressure. Miller explained, "It was like stopping a horse, just dig in your heels and haul back on the reins." Because we felt the Granvilles would have used hydraulic brakes had they been available, modern hydraulic disc brakes were installed with the original size wheel and 10in smooth contour tire. By using the same hinged rudder pedal as the original, the pilot can now operate

Opposite page
Who says an R-2 isn't a controllable airplane? Benjamin demonstrates inverted flight—note where the wing's shadow is falling. *EAA/DeKevin Thornton*

The small side door provides entry and exit. It also served as the emergency exit on the 1932 version; pulling a handle jettisoned the door, leaving the pilot to try to slide out the 2ft-sq opening. *Doc Nichol*

T he R-2 is not so different from other fast airplanes cruising the skies, aside from the fact that you must fly it all the time.

—Delmar Benjamin

the brakes with his toes in the manner of modern airplanes. The tailwheel, which was fixed on the original R-2, was converted to a free-swiveling unit that could be locked straight for takeoffs, landings, or when parked. This is necessary on pavement for maneuvering and turning off the runway after landing.

The only emergency exit route from the original R-2 was through the 2sq-ft side door. As escape through this door would be very difficult, we built the canopy with quick release.

If the pilot needs to leave in a hurry, he ducks his head and pulls the handles. A slightly heavier roll-over structure was added behind the headrest in case the airplane was over-braked or stubbed its wheels and flipped onto its back. Then the quick release on the little side door might prove handy.

We decided on individual exhaust stacks after watching some original newsreel footage of the 1932 Thompson Trophy race. The barking sound of Doolittle's and the other racer's short stacks raised goose bumps.

To avoid any carburetor icing concerns we opted for fuel injection, which needs no heat as only air is passing through the throttle body. Inverted fuel and oil pickup tubes were installed as well. I knew in the back of my mind, with Delmar at the controls, this airplane would be flown inverted.

Getting Out the Hammer and Rock

Our plan was to build the R-2 over a full working year. That was until the world's biggest air show, the Experimental Aircraft Association (EAA) in Oshkosh, Wisconsin, announced that its 1991 theme would be the Golden Age of Air Racing. Would it be possible to build and fly this airplane to Oshkosh, now just nine months away? There were plenty of projects to finish at Wolf Aircraft —a custom aircraft building shop consisting of my wife Liz, shop crew Duane Trappen and Jim McAllister, and myself—before our full-time attention could be devoted to the Gee Bee. But our excitement increased as the available hours decreased, so we decided to go for it.

It's a great credit to the intrepid pilots of that day [early 30s] that anyone could actually take off, fly and land that R-1 without incident. It didn't happen very many times.

—Roger Huntington,
Thompson Trophy Racers

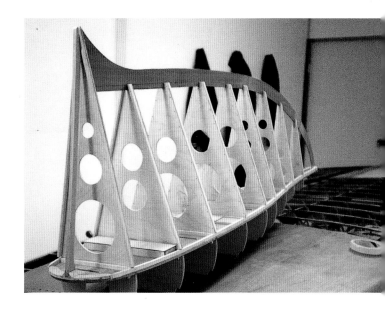

The unusual rudder under construction. After hinge fittings are added, this structure will be covered with 1/16in plywood. The finished rudder is more than 12in wide, extremely rigid, but relatively light. *Steve Wolf*

While Delmar hammered out the wheel streamlines and built the wing ribs in Montana, we got going on the main structure. To complete the R-2 in this short time frame, Wolf Aircraft needed to devote full-time to it. This meant that I could not build the plane as a joint project. The R-2 would instead be built solely for Delmar. From here on out it would be the Benjamin Gee Bee R-2 Replica.

Work began with the rudder, cutting out the ribs, putting on cap strips, and building the spar. When the ribs and trailing edge were glued to the spar, we had a very strange-looking object. As one wag observed, "Looks like it should be floating down the Nile, not on the back of an airplane." The 12in thick rudder did look more like a boat hull than an airplane part. Basically, the airplane's whole back-end moves. The tapering of the fuselage continues straight from the hinge line to the tip of the rudder. Although it looks quite unusual, Miller said it was very effective at both low and high speeds.

The Gee Bee's wheel pants were a project in themselves. Hand-bumped from 0.063in aluminum, as were the originals, they were the first of thousands of items hand-built for the airplane. The basic size and shape was determined by projecting original photographs on a wall, then adjusting the projector-to-wall distance until the correct size was found. Forms were cut from particle board and glued together to create the basic profile, then finished with foam and bondo. We created a female mold by building wooden boxes around the two halves and pouring concrete over them.

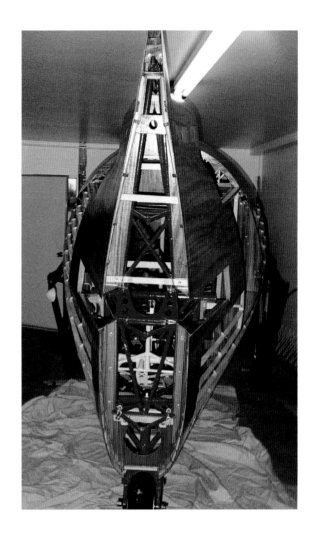

The socket into which the rudder fits, a very difficult part of fitting on this project. There is only a 1/8in gap for rudder movement. Note the slot where the horizontal tail slides in. *Steve Wolf*

Opposite page
The red-knobbed lever, in concert with a matching one on the cockpit's opposite side, jettisons the canopy in an emergency. If needed, you would pull back on both levers, stand up, and jump. There is very little tail to worry about hitting. *Doc Nichol*

The hammering process had not been underway very long before neighbors from all directions were peering over the patio fence to see what the commotion was. Delmar was wintering in Arizona, but to keep the peace he elected to return to his farm in the wilds of Montana to finish hammering the sheets of 6061 aluminum into the mold. It took eight hours of pounding to get the rough shape, and countless hours with a planishing hammer on

The basic horizontal stabilizer under construction. The spars were designed to handle a tail load of 75lb-ft^2 to prevent any chance of flutter. When finished, the stabilizer will be covered with thin mahogany plywood. Even though it has an 8ft span, notice the big gap required for the fuselage. *Steve Wolf*

a dolly to get a smooth surface. Delmar had no previous experience metal bumping and taught himself as he pressed on to each new phase of the project. The halves were welded together, and much time with a body file and sandpaper achieved a perfect surface without resorting to body putty. Finally, the pants were fitted to the gear legs. A 1/4in steel tube was carefully rolled into the bottom of the wheel pants to stiffen and strengthen the wheel opening.

With other customer projects completed, January 1, 1991, marked the day Wolf Aircraft could begin devoting full-time to the R-2. We began by cutting tubing for the fuselage which was engineered to withstand more than 12g. The fuselage's front bay structure was built with 2in diameter chromoly tubing with a 0.095in wall thickness, just like the original. Each side of the fuselage was laid out then tacked together. Looking at the stubby frame, we were sure we must have left out a bay. The basic airframe is only 2in longer than the Pitts Special S-1 frame, yet it's 50in across the front.

Next, we began work on the wing attachment stubs and wings. After the wing broke on the Z model, Zantford Granville said, "There will never be another wing failure on a Gee Bee." The way these R Model wings are built, I'm sure he is right. The wings' front spars are made up of two 1in thick, solid spruce spars laminated together, and the rear spar is 1-1/4in thick. Consequently, the wings are very stout despite being only 4in thick.

The front spars have a 1-1/2in hole drilled through them and the rear spars have a 1-

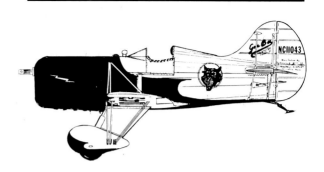

D Model

1/4in hole. High-strength alloy plates, 1/4in thick and 36in long, sandwich both sides of the spars. The heavy-walled compression tubes inserted through the holes in the spars are centered on these plates and are the attachment point for the wing brace wires. Even though Pete Miller had designed the wing not to require drag wires, Granville insisted on using them. Miller said that the wings were originally engineered to 450mph. There's no doubt in my mind they would hang on at that speed if the aileron didn't set up a flutter.

The fuselage frame was finished and sitting proudly on its sturdy gear. The wings were together minus skinning. I've learned that no matter how carefully you build, you should always do a trial assembly. This proved to be a bragging rights moment. Not only did all the fittings line up perfectly, but all bolts slid in with just a gentle tap. The measurements from the tail post to each wingtip proved to be within 1/8in of one another.

The aileron control system is very unique, and it's so simple, most designers wouldn't think of it. The aileron has a torque tube extending out of the root end of the wing. When the wing is slid into place, the torque tube end presses onto a bearing fastened to the fuselage. The control horn (arm) is welded to the torque tube pointing down into the belly. Another arm aiming forward has 6lb of lead bolted to it for balancing the aileron. The control stick is connected to another torque tube running for and aft. It also has an arm pointing down into the belly. A push/pull rod connects these two arms directly, eliminating the need for bellcranks. It's foolproof and works very smoothly.

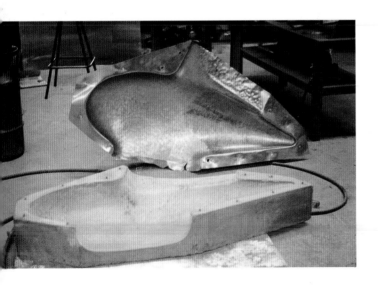

The right half of one wheel streamline after it was planished in the concrete mold shown in the foreground. The streamlines are formed from 0.063in aluminum, then welded together.
Delmar Benjamin

To achieve maximum speed, the Gee Bee used an adjustable horizontal stabilizer operated by a wheel at the leading edge of the pilot's seat. As the pilot rotates the wheel, a jackscrew system moves the rear spar of the stabilizer up or down. The front spar is attached to a pivot point on the fuselage. Once again, it is very simple and it works beautifully.

The rudder and elevators are controlled by cables. Neither of these control surfaces is balanced. Since we knew the airplane would be very responsive in pitch, we set up the joystick so a lot of movement would result in little deflection of the elevators.

Plywood-skinning almost the entire airplane proved interesting. Many people said that we would never get a smooth finish if we used 1/16in mahogany skins like those used on the original Gee Bees; and we did notice some waviness in photos of the original R-2. Master airplane builder Jim Younkin told us that he would float his skins in his swimming pool for days before using them. Since we lacked a pool at the shop, we soaked them down and kept them between sheets of polypropylene. After a minimum of four days, they were ready. Every plywood skin on this airplane is a compound curve (curving two directions at the same time), hence laying them down smoothly was very challenging. With persistence we prevailed. As the moisture evaporated from the skins, they tightened up into smooth, wave-free surfaces.

All the plywood areas were covered with a lightweight Dacron fabric. The fuselage and stringers were covered with a heavier Dacron,

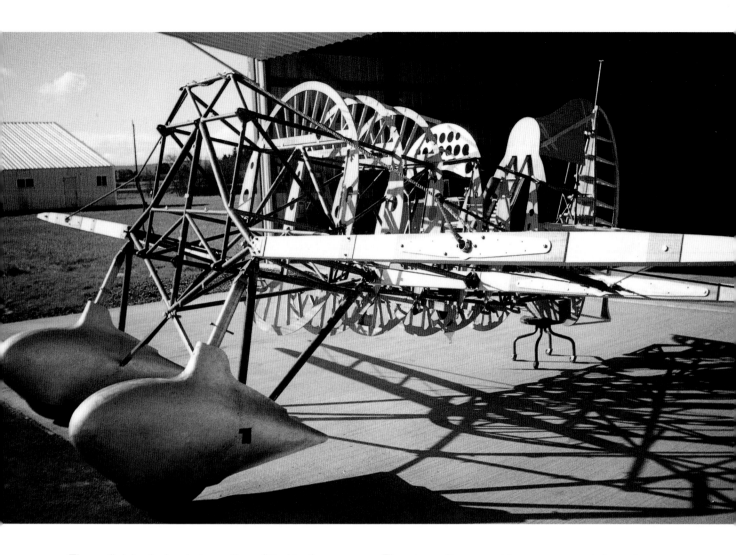

The unfinished wheel streamlines fitted to the gear during one of the many trial assemblies.

The streamlines need to move up and down the gear leg as the shocks work. *Steve Wolf*

and then the entire fuselage was covered with the lightweight material. This gave the R-2 a very smooth, double-strength surface. The fabric weave was then filled with a nitrate dope filler.

We purchased an English wheeling machine for all the compound-curved sheet metal parts. Unfortunately, none of us had ever operated one, but another call to Younkin brought some good pointers. The cowling presented a particularly challenging metal rolling task. It's made up of six side panels that required over forty hours to produce. We hammered out the nose bowl next, rolling a

1/2in steel tube into the leading edge. Some bulkheads were hand-pounded into shape to reinforce the cowl and act as an air deflectors for engine cooling.

A crate showed up from Tulsa Aircraft Engines. There aren't words to describe just how beautiful a R-985 Pratt & Whitney looks after the Tulsa crew have rebuilt it. We knew that the original R-985 the Granvilles had borrowed from Pratt & Whitney didn't have all the chrome and such, but we had to have it.

Norm Taylor had volunteered to make the canopy glass. I made a mold out of sheet aluminum, packaged it up, and sent it to him. When he was done he delivered it air express—in his Cessna.

Laying out the paint scheme was made easy by the accuracy of the Clements-supplied drawings. When I scaled the lines up to full size they lined up perfectly with the stringers, the door, and other reference points.

Gee Bee R-2 Replica Specifications

Wing span	25ft
Wing area	102.2sq-ft
Aspect ratio	6.1
Overall length	17ft 9in
Empty weight	2150lb
Gross weight	3100lb with full fuel
Powerplant	450hp Pratt &Whitney Wasp Jr. 985
Maximum level speed	257mph
Fuel capacity	104gal, two tanks
(66gal front, 38gal rear)	
Oil capacity	6gal
Wing chord at root	53in
Angle of incidence	2.5deg
Dihedral	4.5deg
Maximum fuselage diameter	61in
Wheel tread	76in
Airfoil section	65 percent thick M-6
Horizontal tail span	8ft
Horizontal tail area	15.5sq-ft
Vertical tail area	13.5sq-ft

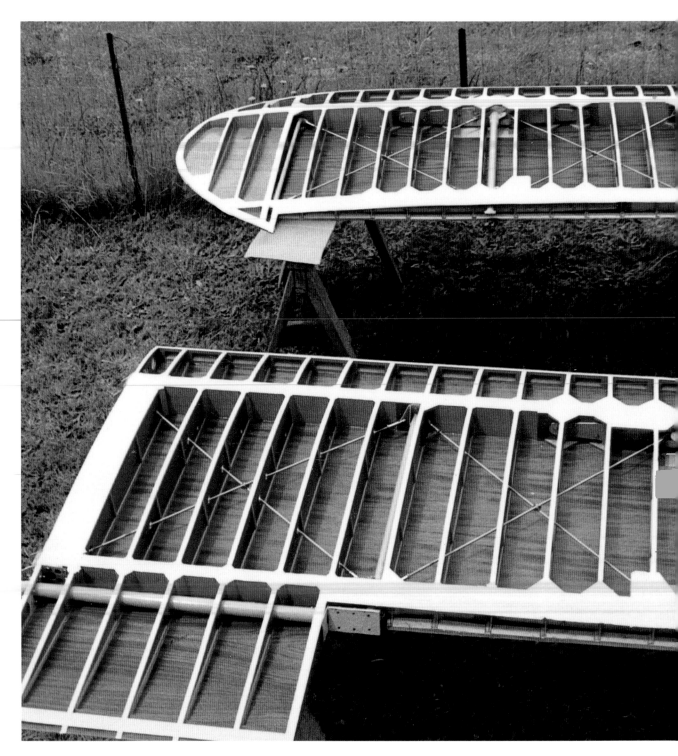

Benjamin was told before the first flight that the airplane could not be sideslipped or banked more than 30 degrees. Within fifteen minutes after take off he had rolled it 360 degrees and sideslipped to a landing.

The wing bottoms have been skinned and varnished and the tops await the same. Notice the torque tube, drag wires, compression tubes, and heavy spars. Though just over 9ft long, these wings feel as if they are carved from solid wood when finished. *Duane Trappen*

The wing was placed in a jig to hold the exact rigging, then skinned with 1/16in plywood. Strips of wood were stapled over the skins to assure a good, tight fit with the ribs. After the skins dried, the strips and staples were removed leaving a smooth plywood surface. *Duane Trappen*

Left
The Gee Bee during trial assembly. Notice the three elevator hinges per side, plus a center hinge. This is an extremely strong airplane, designed to withstand 12g and a 450mph dive speed. Wolf's airshow aircraft, *Samson*, is in the background. *Duane Trappen*

The fuselage ready for cloth cover. The long control stick allows large movements for small amounts of control deflection. The Granvilles felt this would keep pilots from over-controlling the airplane. Notice the horizontal tail pivot bearings. *Steve Wolf*

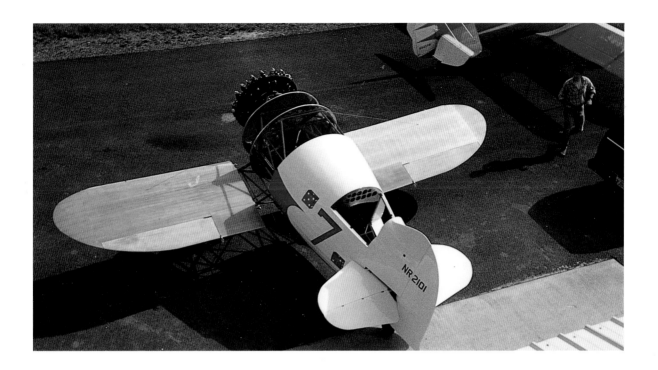

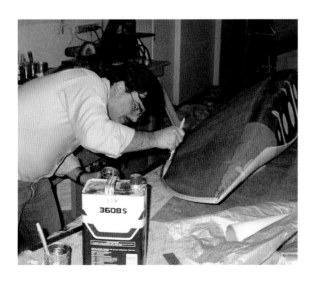

Jim McAllister glues the lightweight cloth covering to the rudder. Once covered, it will then be spray-filled with nitrate dope. The final step is painting: six coats of white polyurethane, followed by the red trim. *Steve Wolf*

Another trial assembly to ensure that all wing wire holes are correctly placed. I've always loved this angle of the Gee Bee. It would be impossible to draw a caricature of this airplane— it already is one. *Steve Wolf*

O ne fellow told Delmar, "You know this thing isn't going to fly." Delmar asked, "How can you walk by the Stealth Fighter and then come over here and tell me this won't fly?"

T

he landing gear's forward thrust gives the R-2 a silhouette not unlike that of a bird of prey.

Each panel, many compound curved, was hand-built and fit. We wanted to use the same materials as they had in the 1930s and felt that using fiberglass would have been cheating.
Doc Nichol

Chapter 3

Oshkosh, 1991

As the end of July approached, we realized that we weren't going to meet our goal of flying the R-2 to Oshkosh. The big, orange Allied Van Lines truck showed up the Thursday before the EAA Convention, and as we watched it roll north on I-5 with the R-2 in it, I had a personal feeling of failure. This didn't last long, however, as there was still plenty of work to be done before we could head east. The cowling still needed to be riveted together and painted.

After a long day of riveting and with the paint still wet, Delmar loaded the cowl into a small U-Haul trailer. I climbed into my air show airplane, *Samson*, and headed off to Oshkosh. As the Grand Teton mountains passed under my lower wings, I envisioned elliptical white wings with red scallops and a number 7 painted on them. I felt what it must have been like in the 1930s, just you, your airplane, and the drone of the big Pratt & Whitney.

On arriving at Oshkosh, I taxied to the EAA Foundation hanger. Six Allied Van Lines trucks with replica and original racers from all over the country were there. This would be the biggest gathering of these famous race planes since the 1930s.

The Golden Age of Air Racing display was a hit. Hundreds of thousands came by and walked around the Gee Bee. Delmar and his wife Tana spent countless hours answering questions and listening to endless stories of the dreaded Gee Bees. I recall one fellow telling Delmar,"You know this thing isn't going to fly." Looking up from his lawn chair Delmar asked, "How can you walk by the Stealth

Opposite page
Two majestic machines from the past sit side-by-side at Oshkosh, 1992. The big, round engines spoke of times past, taking many old timers that knew the originals back to the days of their youth. *EAA/DeKevin Thornton*

Loading the big Gee Bee for the trip to the EAA's 1991 air show in Oshkosh, Wisconsin.
Steve Wolf

it." After hours of sanding, we clear-coated the wings to give them that super-gloss look.

The wing and tail fairings were hand-hammered much like the wheel pants, with the exception of fiberglass molds used for the aft section of the wing root. The horizontal tail faring proved to be quite intricate in nature due to the movable stabilizer. As the stabilizer moves vertically it must also slide in and out to match the fuselage curve. This dictates that the fairing must float, which is accomplished by using five springs to hold the fairing tight against the fuselage and stabilizer.

With most of the work finished, it was time to get the R-2 inspected and certified for airworthiness. The FAA has set up several retired maintenance inspectors as Designated Airworthiness Representatives (DAR). They still retain their authority to inspect and issue airworthiness certificates. On December 21, 1991, Keith Antcliff flew his Beech A-36 down from Spokane, bringing with him DAR Lee Dubay, and aviation enthusiasts Jack Rose and Dick Atwood. Everyone dug into the remaining work, and they were a big help in

Fighter and then come over here and tell me that this won't fly?"

Finishing What We Started

Once all the pieces had returned from Oshkosh, it was time to start bolting things together permanently. The big push for Oshkosh was over, but we set a new goal. If the R-2 took to the air before the year's end, we would have built it in under one year. I took on the building of the fuel tanks and plumbing, while Delmar started the wing root filets.

With only 75sq-ft of actual wing area, we wanted each square inch to give maximum lift. Consequently, many hours were spent sanding them to a hand-rubbed finish. Granville had enlisted a group of school kids to sand the original's wings telling them, "I want it so smooth that a fly will slide off if he lands on

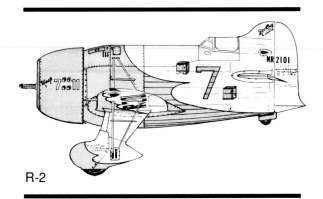

R-2

completing our goal of flying the R-2 before 1991 ended.

By the morning of the December 22, word had gotten out that the Gee Bee might fly before sunset. Dozens of people stood just outside the open hangar door, while others came in and asked to help. You couldn't help but feel that history would soon be relived, and no one wanted to miss it.

With the sun now low on the horizon and the winter chill setting in, I thought the spectators would leave. Not so. They hung around to see the big barrel-shaped airplane lifted onto the scales. It was at this moment, with the R-2 sitting tall on the scales, that I realized what we had created. It was amazing to realize that the original airplane had sat at this stage only twenty-nine years after the Wright brothers first flew.

Delmar decided not to disappoint the crowd that had so patiently waited all day. The cool, night air was broken by applause as the R-2 was rolled out. I hand-cranked the Pratt & Whitney to life. Smoke puffed from the stacks, followed closely by the sound of exploding fuel. Delmar gunned the engine and flames shot out all around the cowl's trailing edge. There was an equal roar from the spectators. He taxied the big Gee Bee around in front of the hangar, spun it in little circles, and blasted the throttle, exciting everyone. I stood directly behind and could see the firing order of the engine as quick flashes of fire shot out. As the hangar door went down, most headed off, but we stayed to listen to the engine creak as it cooled down.

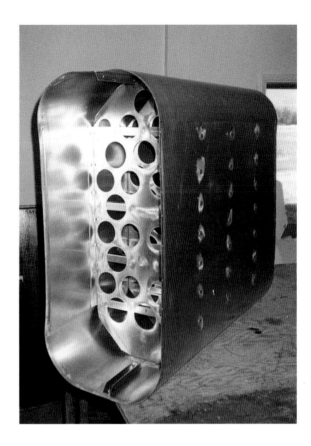

The 38gal main fuel tank sits low in the fuselage between the main landing gear. The forward auxiliary fuel tank, shown here, holds 66gal. Interior baffling adds much needed structural strength and prevents the fuel from sloshing around. Under normal flying conditions, the total fuel capacity of 104gal is enough to stay aloft for four hours. At full race power, however, the Pratt & Whitney will consume all fuel in less than two hours. *Steve Wolf*

The Dream Comes True

December 23, 1991, is a date I'll always remember. Some high clouds, no wind or rain. Since this was a Monday, I thought the number of spectators would be minimal, but nearly everyone from the day before returned, following the Gee Bee from the hangar to the gas pumps. After one more preflight, it was time to find out which stories were true.

Delmar, having what he hoped wasn't his last Pepsi, walked over to the Gee Bee and said, "I wanna go fly." Keith Antcliff had agreed to fly chase in his Beech and would carry video and still cameras. With only 3,000ft of runway and no radio in the R-2, the chase plane's pilot would do the radio work for a landing at the controlled Eugene airport if there was an emergency. Antcliff asked Delmar for an emergency signal, and Delmar replied,

The front hand-hammered wing root fillet during the fitting stages. Note the many Clecos (removable fasteners) holding the fairings to the wing and fuselage. Flush screws will replace the Clecos after the fairings are painted. *Steve Wolf*

Onlookers crowd into the hangar as the Gee Bee is scaled. It weighed in at 2,115lb with engine oil. *Doc Nichol*

"If you see flames trailing out past the tail, then I'm having an emergency." As Delmar was strapping into the Gee Bee, Lee Dubay said, "Now you be careful." Delmar answered, "If I were careful, I wouldn't have built a Gee Bee." People lined the runway from one end to the other, each with an idea of which visual angle would provide the best view of the take-off.

Lined up on the runway center line, tail-wheel locked, Delmar and the R-2 started rolling. My heart pounded. The Gee Bee accelerated in tandem with the Pratt & Whitney's roar. This was the first time we had

45

The shining R-985 Pratt & Whitney's individual exhaust stacks are pointing back toward the cowling's trailing edge. Tulsa Aircraft Engines gets credit for the excellent rebuild. The 66gal fuel tank is just aft of the firewall. *Doc Nichol*

heard it at full power. I was standing at the runway's halfway point, and as it went by I saw light under the wheels. Lots of black smoke trailed from the stacks as it was running somewhat rich. As the big Gee Bee crossed the far end of the runway it hit me, I'm seeing a Gee Bee fly. The sound of the R-2 circling over the airport was true music from sixty years ago.

Delmar rolled the R-2 from side to side, checking the aileron response. Then, as I knew he would, he rolled the Gee Bee. A high-speed pass across the field was Antcliff's signal to take off and join the Gee Bee. Delmar shot by the Beech like it was parked.

T he aileron control system is very unique, and it's so simple, most designers wouldn't think of it. . . . It's foolproof and works very smoothly.

—Steve Wolf

I t's ironic that these stubby Gee Bee designs that proved to be such man-killers had more "educated" design in them than many more conventional ships.

—Roger Huntington,
Thompson Trophy Racers

Coming around and joining the Beech, Delmar rolled the Gee Bee inverted just 30ft off its wing. I then knew that the R-2 was a controllable airplane.

There isn't any way to describe the feelings I had that day. I saw an R-Model Gee Bee fly in my lifetime. It was made possible by the dedication of many people—too numerous to mention. Some 6,000 hours of our lives went into creating this airplane. Now I knew it was all worth it. Delmar probably said it best when he stepped out of the Gee Bee after the first flight and said, "Now that's an airplane."

47

"If you build it they will come." Wherever the Gee Bee goes, the crowds follow. *Doc Nichol*

Previous pages
Lining-up for takeoff. As evidenced by this photo, the view forward is nil for the first few seconds of the roll. The pilot must be assured that the runway is clear before takeoff or landing. *EAA/Jim Koepnick*

Right
Model builders and flyers had a good knowledge of the Gee Bee's flight characteristics, finding it controllable in the air but a challenge to land. It behaved just the same in full scale. *EAA/Mike Steineke*

The first flight. This photo was taken from the chase airplane which was serving as the Gee Bee's communication link. Catching a glimpse of the horizontal tail out of the corner of his eyes, Benjamin said he thought his airplane was trying to pass him. The headrest is only 28in in front of the rudder. *Lee Dubay*

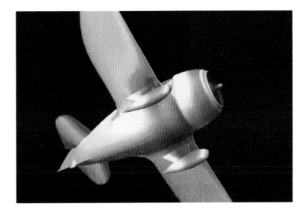

Computer-generated surface pressure graphics. The color scale on the photo above indicates the coeffecient of pressure. Blue indicates the highest pressure and magenta the lowest. Yellow represents ambient pressure. *David A. Lednicer*

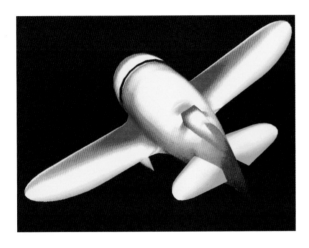

Left
Due to the teardrop shape, every panel on the R-2 is a compound curve. This complexity added hundreds of hours to the construction time. *Ray Conkling*

The chase pilot asked Delmar for an emergency signal. Delmar replied, "If you see flames trailing out past the tail, then I'm having an emergency."

Chapter 4

First Flight

Flying the R Model Gee Bee has been a most challenging and enjoyable experience. It is quite impossible to relate the excitement of flying this happy little racer through a pen.

Although I did not strike out to achieve the Gee Bee, looking back, I can see that I unconsciously sailed a fairly straight course to it. I committed my full attention to the project in November 1989, liquidating all of my air show assets to raise capital. Thereafter, every spare minute went into achieving the R-2. Although I am technically the R-2's test pilot, it seems more like stepping into a dream world than piloting an actual piece of machinery. I flew the Gee Bee a thousand times in the simulator between my ears before December 23, 1991, and in reality it performed in all aspects just as in the simulator.

The test flight was not a major undertaking for me, but rather just a small step up from the simulator to the cockpit. I sold my previous airplane in 1989, and I had only flown twice between then and the first Gee Bee flight, but I had no doubt that my reflexes would fly the airplane just as they enabled me to ride a bicycle and drive a car. There is no airplane in existence that I feel would have prepared me for the flight of the Gee Bee better than the mental exercises I went through thousands of times before the actual flight.

On the day of the test flight, I approached the task with the determination of a samurai going into battle. Lift off was rather abrupt due to an aft CG and lack of elevator pressure, and the aircraft headed uphill more quickly than I desired. Grasping the stick firmly with both hands, I stopped porpoising after about

Opposite page
The Gee Bee on short final. A slight sideslip and a steep angle permits an adequate view of the runway until the tail comes down. *EAA/Mike Steineke*

Liftoff is not attempted until 120mph is attained. Once the tail is up the view forward is greatly improved. Acceleration during takeoff is quite rapid—0 to 140mph in about 1,000ft. *Jay Tolbert*

three oscillations. Once stabilized, I relaxed and flew the climb out with two fingers. The words of Jimmy Doolittle echoed in my mind, "The R Model must be flown with silk gloves and is likened to balancing a pencil on the end of your finger." Words of wisdom! I would add that silk shoes would also be to the pilot's advantage. Very minuscule movement of the rudders resulted in the pilot careening between the longerons, as he sits with his back virtually against the tail post. The rate of climb stayed pegged at 4000fpm.

Benjamin and the R-2 just prior to the first flight. *Dave Schwartz*

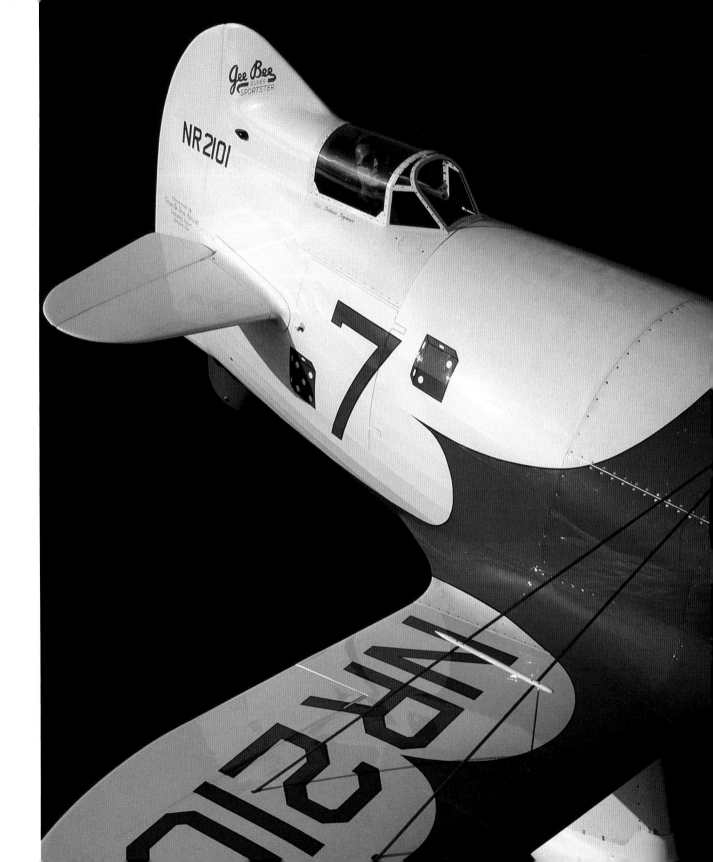

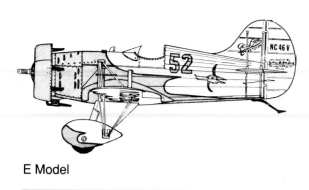

E Model

After a couple of orbits of the Creswell, Oregon, airfield, I was comfortable enough to explore slow flight. Accompanying any power reduction under 160mph, the landing wires set up a vibration turning the wire stays into a 6in blur. As the little airplane passed through 100mph, the nose dropped as if I'd run off a cliff. There was no tendency to drop a wing, and my reflex to wake up the 500 horses brought it back to flying speed

Right
The first flight of the R-2 was over the beautiful Willamette Valley south of Eugene, Oregon. Final R-2 assembly had been performed near there at Wolf Aircraft in Creswell, Oregon. *Ray Conkling*

Previous page
This in-flight close-up shows the superb workmanship that went into the R-2 replica. Pete Miller has commented that the replica is much better finished than the original. *Ray Conkling*

directly. Next in my adventure was to explore the ailerons. I was pleased to find the pressures and roll rate comparable to the Pitts Special—delightful!

Looping maneuvers proved somewhat less happy as the duration at high speed with no or negative elevator pressure constantly tried to put me to sleep with 6g positive and negative oscillations.

After about fifteen minutes of familiarizing myself with my little plane, the chase pilot began his climb for the air-to-air camera work. The plan was to get as many photos as possible in case I failed to bring the R-2 back in one piece. Also, the chase plane was to be my communication with the tower—the R-2 had no radio—should I need to use the longer runway in Eugene.

During the chase plane's climb, I accelerated the Gee Bee to 250mph, and made a low high-speed pass. There is no real sensation of speed from the cockpit; the Pratt & Whitney just thumps away at any speed. Accounts from the ground are somewhat different as the aircraft approaches with a glorious Gee Bee scream and staccato exhaust music.

After several laps in knife-edge and inverted flight I was ready to come down. In the excitement preceding the first flight I left my earplugs in my pocket, and after thirty minutes sitting behind those short stacks I was really ready to come down.

I flew the downwind leg of the landing pattern at 180mph, turning to final speed bleeds to 160mph. I slipped in over the trees at about 140mph with a touchdown at

120mph. The rudder loses effectiveness at considerable speed, so I had to use differential braking to finish the roll. This last phase of the landing was more akin to wrestling than to rolling and was one of the things for which I needed to reprogram myself.

With each new flight I became more infatuated with the ship and gained more respect for the courageous souls straddling the sticks sixty years ago. I also discovered a few idiosyncrasies of the aircraft that needed to be fixed or worked around. I had no desire to change the configuration of the airframe or try to improve it with a fatter airfoil, more wing, or improved visibility. If I did, it would lose the essence of the Gee Bee. Instead, I wanted to master the beast in its original configuration and enjoy it for the neat little character that it is.

The items I felt had to be fixed were CG location, the seat restraints, landing wire vibration, and braking methods. The seat was easily fixed by adding wraparound hip restraints. Stays were added to the landing wires as on the original. An optimum CG location at 18 percent of the chord was recommended by Curtis Pitts. This would improve pitch and rudder sensitivity. Although we chose the best brakes available, they are a weak link that we will have to work around. In trying to improve my landings, I made four full stops and takeoffs in a row. On the last roll out the brake

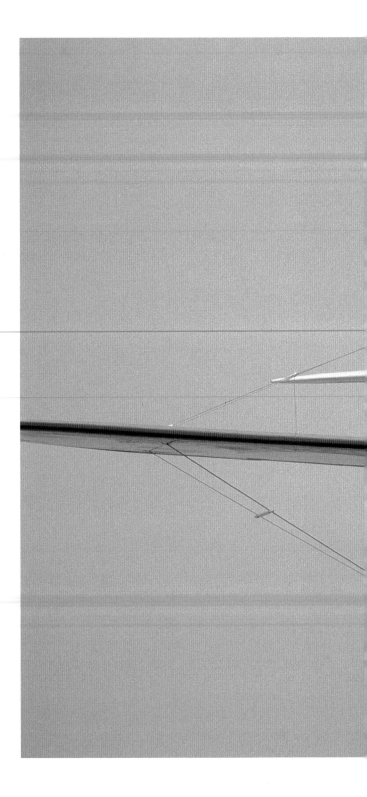

A high speed pass by the R-2 is an exhilarating experience for those on the ground. The Gee Bee screams by at close to 300mph on a fast pass. *EAA/Jim Koepnick*

calipers melted and the peddles went to the stops. In talking with Parker-Cleveland engineers, we discovered that brakes are designed to stop one time and then be allowed to cool. This is a problem I will have to manage by minimum brake use. Losing the brakes means losing the airplane, as it depends on them to steer through the final roll out.

The biggest flight characteristics discovery was a phenomenon that I personally believe led to the demise of the original R Models and was also prevalent in the Hall Bull Dog: the tendency for aileron reversal at high angles of attack and near stall speed. I encountered this nasty gremlin on the third landing. Having seen film of the original aircraft landing three point, I got the tail down at a fairly good speed so I could use the brakes hard. As we drifted to the right, I fed in left aileron and rudder at a speed well under the stall at altitude, and the right wing abruptly lost lift and dropped. This in turn pitched the left wing up and it flew quite well, popping me up into a knife-edge landing. Fortunately, I got the tail up and arrested the snap roll before we cartwheeled down the runway. I will be eternally grateful that I discovered this phenomenon and did not destroy the airplane. Hereafter,

The symmetrical aileron on the Gee Bee is very effective with a roll rate comparable to a Pitts. Stick forces are light at all speeds. *Ray Conkling*

P eople have hinted that the R-2 is too valuable to be flown. I feel it is too valuable not to be flown and I am honored to give the Gee Bee the chance to shine that it was denied in its first life in 1932.

—Delmar Benjamin

the tail stays up until we slow to a fast run. The aerodynamics of the problem are that the aileron deflections change the angle of attack of the airfoil, increasing one side while decreasing the other. This, aggravated by the nose-high attitude in a three point, results in a snap roll at some narrow band on the airspeed. I intend to avoid this landing configuration at all costs!

Following pages
Benjamin's learning curve was very steep for the Gee Bee's first few flights. Although he had a rough idea how the airplane would handle, the reality was that until the throttle was opened no living pilot—excepting Jimmy Doolittle—really knew how the machine would fly. *Jim Koepnick*

Chapter 5

The Gee Bee on the Air Show Circuit

Awaiting my turn to fly at the 1992 Cleveland National Air Show (home of the original 1932 Thompson Trophy race), a thousand thoughts race through my head. As my turn gets closer I stop noticing the crowd's excitement and begin concentrating on the Gee Bee and the job at hand. The show boss will want me on stage within one or two minutes.

I usually do a walk-around inspection at this point to make sure all is in order with the aircraft. Enough fuel has to be on board to fly the routine and perhaps hold for a short time. Not too much fuel can be added or the CG will move aft into the danger zone and the wing loading will go up, raising the stall speed even higher. I give special attention to a few critical items including the prop, cowling, and flying wires. In addition to a final check of the airframe, the touching and tugging tends to calm me and instill confidence in the machine. Once the throttle is opened and the wings begin to create lift, all thoughts of the machine disappear and it becomes an extension of my own being.

As an athlete gives little thought to muscle and bone during the heat of competition, so does a pilot forget wires and spars. All attention is focused on the show line (an FAA-required imaginary line which maintains a 500ft distance between show planes and all spectators and property), obstacles in the area, and energy management of the flight. Energy management is basically a combination of velocity and height above the ground. As you lose one you must exchange it for the other. This becomes more critical with higher altitudes and thinner air. In addition to the loss of

Opposite page
Benjamin rounds pylon number two at 1992's Reno Air Races. A speed of 279mph was clocked on this trip around the T-6 course. *Alfred J. Manley*

Benjamin hefts the 1932 Thompson Trophy. The original R-1 won 1932's race with Jimmy Doolittle at the controls. Lee Gehlbach finished fifth in the R-2. *Sid Bradd*

lift at altitude, the horsepower of the engine also decreases, making it more difficult to maintain speed.

With the exception of a quick glance at the oil temperature and airspeed, all my attention is on the environment of the show line. I must compensate for wind at all times to avoid overflying the crowd or the next county. This day at Cleveland, sea gulls are of some concern as a T-38 had ingested some previously and had gone into Lake Erie.

The most difficult maneuver in my routine by far is the landing. So far I have executed every landing safely, but only due to a great deal of concentration. During the air show routine I remain in a calm and comfortable state, but upon entering the landing mode I push upright in the seat and acquire a samurai's determination. As the sensation of speed dissipates and the world winds down, the samurai exhales a long held breath and Delmar slowly returns to the polished red leather seat. The focus of the flight broadens, and once again the excitement of the crowd returns.

Reno Air Races

The excitement generated by speed and pylons was as strong at Reno 1992 as it was sixty years ago at the 1932 Cleveland air races. The Gee Bee roared around the course with speeds from 252mph to 279mph depending on the length of the downhill run to the starting line.

On one run down the chute, the air speed approached 300mph, the highest speed attained by the replica. Reno's spectators are some of the most dedicated fans you will find anywhere. Gee Bee fever struck as the crowd gathered around the R-2 in the pits, and the huge inventory of Gee Bee T-shirts was sold out by Sunday morning.

Tiger Destefani and his modified Mustang, *Strega*, won the gold in 1992. The progress made in piston-driven aircraft was reflected in *Strega's* lap speed, over 200mph faster than the R-2 could muster.

Benjamin awaits his turn to fly at the Cleveland National Air Show. *Deltana Airshows, Inc.*

One of the few times Benjamin can clearly see the runway—fortunately landing isn't on the agenda. *Jay Tolbert*

Right
Inverted and probably no more than 20ft off the deck, the Gee Bee clips the ribbon at about 270mph. *Jay Tolbert*

T he words of Jimmy Doolittle echoed in my mind, "The R model must be flown with silk gloves and is likened to balancing a pencil on the end of your finger."

—Delmar Benjamin

Left
Pylon turns are what the Gee Bee was designed to do. Visibility in racing configuration is excellent. *EAA/Mike Steineke*

At speeds greater than 200mph indicated, the tail is high enough to allow the pilot to see over the nose. Unfortunately, the speeds during takeoff and landing are always less, and the view forward disappears. *EAA/Jim Koepnick*

Sixty years of air racing. *Strega*, the 1992 Reno
unlimited winner, posing with the Gee Bee.
Frank Gurko

Left
The Gee Bee a split second past pylon number
two at the 1992 Reno Air Races. *Alfred J.
Manley*

There is no real sensation of
speed from the cockpit; the
Pratt & Whitney just thumps away
at any speed.

—Delmar Benjamin

The R-2's unique cockpit location takes some getting used to. Benjamin says he often feels as if the airplane's tail surfaces are trying to pass him. *EAA/Phil High*

Cross-country runs at speeds up to 250mph are the Gee Bee's forte—if the weather is good. *Ray Conkling*

Spirit of the R-2

My interpretation of the Gee Bee's life is probably quite different than that which would be related by an air show fan or a historian. For me the Gee Bee world is a place of vivid contrast, where great danger and great beauty come together. To enter this world one must be alert and concentrated. While in this state of awareness the senses are very keen and perceptive to the environment. The combination of thrill and beauty tends to create a false sense of safety and security when in reality disaster might be only a heartbeat away.

A moment in the Gee Bee's life that I feel captures these sensations occurred on my journey home from the East Coast from yet another air show. Rising at dawn, I had flown hard to make it home in one, long day. This moment found the Gee Bee and me 300 miles from home with the sun just hovering above the horizon.

I had just topped off the fuel so I could run at full power in a race with the sun. The airplane was really in its element here, indicating 250mph on a cross-country run, just as Pete Miller had designed it to do. The line of thunderstorms I had been watching on the horizon now towered 30,000ft above us and squalls were blowing up dust on the surface. The clear spaces between storms were closing fast and would soon become a wall of rain and hail. The highway I had been following disappeared into the center of a large storm cell.

In any other aircraft I would have retreated to safety, but the samurai spirit of the Gee Bee made me press on to complete the race. Slower and more fragile craft would surely fail, but this one raced on in a contest with the thunder gods. Exhaust stains streaked back from the cowl, gracefully arching over the airfoil and curling under the stabilizer, like a footprint of the lift extracted from the passing wind. Joining the exhaust stains were drops of oil from the laboring Pratt & Whitney, stretched taut by the steady gale.

In the midst of this battle I sat calmly, intent on the storms and the setting sun. On the horizon lay home, a meal, and a warm bed. We squeezed between the Bear Paw Mountains and the menacing, towering cumulus. The empty wheat fields counted off the miles as I raced along. I kept the altitude to a minimum, partly because the engine developed more power that way and partly due to the feeling of speed it gave me. As the Bear Paw Mountains slid by the left wing with cloud bases topping the peaks, the Rocky Mountains shone under clear skies 200 miles ahead with the sun sinking into the snow-capped summit. The Blackfoot Indians called them the shining mountains, and it was easy to see why from my perspective at that moment.

I believe I have given the Gee Bee the chance to shine that it was denied in 1932. The airplane performs at air shows to pay its way, but its true gratification comes from pressing hard across the country as it was designed to do in the Bendix Trophy race of sixty years past.

Storm clouds threaten, but the Gee Bee remains undaunted. *EAA/Jim Koepnick*

Overflying primitive terrain can cause some anxiety if much thought is given to an engine failure. The speed and glide ratio of the Gee Bee are not conducive to off-airport landings. *Ray Conkling*

Chapter 6

The Gee Bee in Restrospect

Since the first flight on December 23, 1991, I have learned a great deal about the Gee Bee. Flying the airplane around the Creswell Airport in the pattern I described earlier was a far cry from traveling the North American continent. My most intense anxiety was setting out across the mountains into uncertain weather, rather than the traditional white-knuckle Gee Bee stories history has impressed on us. Looking back, I believe that after six or so flights I had a pretty good handle on landing and takeoff technique. I have aborted only one landing and I haven't had any bad ones yet, although every landing is a very intense exercise.

Just when I thought I had mastered the landing routine, I was snapped back to reality. In April 1992, I found myself in a part of Kansas where all the runways were north and south and the wind was at 270 degrees, gusting to 20 knots. As I crabbed down the chute on final, I couldn't help but wonder if this was where Dorothy and Toto disappeared. The Gee Bee has a huge side area, actually about 30sq-ft more than wing area, so crosswinds are a challenge. The high landing speed makes the problem manageable on touchdown, but it becomes somewhat of a wrestling match under 80mph. Thanks to the effective brakes and a mad dance on the peddles it all worked out and I stayed on the runway.

My only criticism of the airplane mechanically is its annoying tendency to spit out an exhaust stack periodically. On a trip to Florida for the Sun 'n Fun Air Show, I lost two stacks completely and welded up five cracked ones.

Opposite page
Benjamin discovered on the first flight that the airplane flew knife-edge better than any airplane he had ever flown. This characteristic is due to the large fuselage area and airfoil shape. *Ray Conkling*

Benjamin and #7 covered a lot of ground during the summer of 1992. The racer was demonstrated for 3.5 million spectators around the country. *Ray Conkling*

Thus far, I have only described the Gee Bee's general mechanical behavior, but I can't leave out the surrealistic side of this experience. It is very easy to slip back to 1932 while flying across this big country. I often find myself pondering the landscape as Lee Gehlbach would have seen it some sixty years ago.

Because of the Gee Bee's ability to transport me back in time, I was able to solve a mystery concerning Lee Gehlbach and the Bendix Trophy race. I often wondered why the early Bendix racers went via Albuquerque and not direct from Burbank to Cleveland. After leaving Oshkosh in August 1992, I headed for a show at Salt Lake City.

It took several attempts before I punched out of the marginal IFR (Instrument Flight

The Gee Bee's paint scheme was inspired by the Coca-Cola signs of the 1930s. Perhaps the airplane's Coke bottle shape played a part in color selection as well. *Ray Conkling*

Rules) conditions at Oshkosh. Then as I approached the western end of Nebraska myriad new problems presented themselves. First, head winds were cutting my range, and second, the surface temperatures exceeded 100 degrees. As the terrain rose into the Rockies these small conditions slowly became big ones. Because of shortened range, I knew I would need fuel somewhere in Wyoming. My choices looked like Rawlings or Rock Springs, which have elevations close to 7,000ft above sea level. With temperatures of 100 degrees I calculated a density altitude of over 11,000ft. With crosswinds from the south at close to 20mph these choices did not appear good to me. I've become accustomed to the high landing speed of the Gee Bee, but with 11,000ft density altitude, the runways go by very quickly with the flippers giving up and the

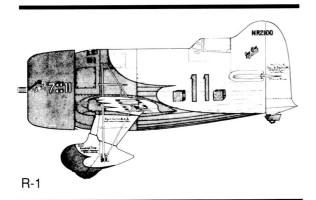

R-1

Crash!

by Lee Gehlbach, *Air Trails* 1939

It has always been a great temptation to put smaller wings on the racers, let the landing speeds be what they may. In 1932 I flew a Gee Bee in the Bendix Transcontinental Race. When I landed in the thin air of the high altitude of Amarillo, Texas, I actually sat down, coming in on the ground at about 150mph. When loaded with gas for the long hop to Cleveland, the airplane needed about 200mph in order to take off. Fortunately, the Amarillo airport has a runway of over two miles—and we needed most of it. Jimmy Doolittle had a sister ship with a larger engine, so he set a new land plane speed record and won the Thompson Trophy race that year.

Lee Gehlbach and the original R-2, 1932. *Sid Bradd*

Although these airplanes were noble experiments, Jimmy and I both considered they were too hot for anybody to handle. We believed that we had used up a considerable portion of our earthly share of luck. We never even sat in them again. We really didn't consider ourselves any more skillful than the boys who later crashed these jobs. Our guardian angels had just stood by us in our hour of need.

Neither of these two airplanes afterwards ever finished a race. Their score was five wrecks and two men. Jimmy Haizlip was just about to land one when a wingtip snapped into the ground. For a miracle, Jimmy was able to walk out of the wreckage with only a few scratches and sore spots and surprised expression on his face. Russell Thaw had one of these jobs behave the same way, but luckily he only tore up a wing before the plane flopped back to roll on its wheels. Yes, those Gee Bees were jinx ships. Roy Minor had just made a good landing with a mile of airport before him. But the grass was wet. Then he locked his brakes. But he was still sliding merrily along when he ran out of airport. The airport remained intact and so did Roy, but the airplane needed a complete rebuilding. During Roy's lifetime, he did some of the greatest racing and hardest flying that has been done. But he died of pneumonia in 1934. While taking off, Russell Boardman had one of these famous Gee Bee's flop over on its back, then slide along the ground, upside-down, for about a thousand feet. It was claimed that this did not kill him; he lived for a couple of days with a fractured skull. Cecil Allen scattered himself and the last hot Gee Bee. He had tried to take off with a big load of gasoline for the Bendix Transcontinental Race.

tail coming down at a very high ground speed.

Shuffling through my maps, I determined the only runway pointing into the wind was Scotts Bluff, Nebraska. It feels very good at times to be down and stopped with the Gee Bee, and this was definitely one of those times. Although I would miss the paycheck and Saturday's show in Salt Lake, they weren't worth risking the Gee Bee (and myself). As I laid in a motel room and waited for conditions to improve, it slowly became apparent to me why the heavily loaded Bendix racers avoided this 7,000ft terrain.

Landing approach is flown at 160mph. *Ray Conkling*

I had landed my heavily loaded Pitts in the wilds of Wyoming at 9,000ft asl after an engine failure, but it had a 12lb wing loading compared with 40lb in the Gee Bee. The Gee Bee flies quite nicely with its 450 horses at work, but when I pull the power lever back it takes on the flight characteristics of a cast iron frisbee. It is a delight to fly when all that power is dragging it around, but that engine is just another 600lb of ballast on landing. Lightly loaded at sea level, with a large runway, the thing is actually fun to land, but above 4,000ft asl it becomes less than enjoyable.

The R-2 is not so different from other fast airplanes cruising the skies, aside from the fact that you must fly it all the time. It is fairly stable in roll and can be trimmed up in pitch with full tanks, but as fuel is burned and the CG moves aft it becomes ever more pitch sensitive.

Its most interesting characteristic is its total divergent tendency in yaw. In smooth clear air I noticed the nose hunting from side to side and my feet pedaling rhythmically to hold a heading. Being of a curious nature I wondered what would happen if I just let it have its way. Removing my feet from the pedals I found it swings side to side, accelerating

The spirit of the R-2—instilled by the Granvilles—is cross-country racing. Pushing hard all day at full power with a minimum of fuel stops is the what this airplane was designed to do. The original R-2 carried 300gal of fuel, a quantity equal to the weight of the unladen airplane. *Ray Conkling*

Right
The Gee Bee provides a surrealistic mode of transportation. Cruising at four miles per minute, it can beat airline connections in crossing the country. *Ray Conkling*

The landing gear's forward thrust gives the R-2 a silhouette not unlike that of a bird of prey. This husky, aggressive stance has captured the imagination of aviation enthusiasts for six decades. *Ray Conkling*

Left
Flying the Gee Bee cross-country in clear weather is very enjoyable, white-knuckle time occurs on landing or fighting bad weather. *Ray Conkling*

Benjamin was told before the first flight that the airplane could not be sideslipped or banked more than 30 degrees. Within fifteen minutes after take off he had rolled it 360 degrees and sideslipped to a landing. Most of the horror stories about the R-models proved to be myth. *EAA/Jim Koepnick*

the tempo with each swing. After about five oscillations, I was clutching the longerons and thrashing about with my feet to stop the wild ride. If I let it go for much longer I probably would have been knocked cold by the canopy.

The Gee Bee is not a good scud running airplane due to its poor forward visibility and high speed. Though flying in poor conditions becomes a way of life in the air show business, I don't leave the ground unless conditions are forecast VFR (Visual Flight Rules). For myself, there is no greater honor than to set out across

the northern Rockies with clear skies and 20-knot tail winds. Under these conditions, that polished red leather seat feels more like a throne, and I wish the moment would last for ever. Unfortunately, the better I feel, the farther forward the throttle advances and all too soon the 100 gallons of fuel on board is converted to artsy soot gracefully curving down the length of the fuselage.

People have hinted that the R-2 is too valuable to be flown. I feel it is too valuable not to be flown and I am honored to give the

Left
Due to its unique aerodynamic characteristics, the R-2 has divergent stability which means it must be flown at all times. Jimmy Doolittle stated that if the controls were released the Gee Bee would attempt to destroy itself. Benjamin concurs with this analysis. *EAA/Jim Koepnick*

Benjamin and Gary Thompson admire the fully-developed exhaust stains. Eventually, the two lower pipes were run together. *Doc Nichol*

Gee Bee the chance to shine that it was denied in its first life in 1932.

Gee Bee Fans

Looking back on the project, I am quite amazed. When we first began on the Gee Bee project, we intended to prove it really did fly and maybe attempt to put 100 hours on it before it went into a museum. When I arrived home after my last air show performance in 1992, the tach showed 145 hours, over 100 more than the original accumulated during its entire life. Looking back through the calendar I count fifty-three performances for an estimated 3.5 million people. The response to the airplane has been better than I ever dreamed. We have shipped posters and videos to twenty countries so far. Virtually every aviation magazine in the world requested information and photos that first summer.

During July 1992, the Gee Bee and I traveled to Bradley Field in the Springfield area so Pete Miller could see the R-2 in the air after

sixty years. To my surprise, a large number of Granvilles were on hand as well. Although we had heard that the Granvilles didn't want another R Model built because of its dangerous characteristics, they were actually quite excited and supportive of the project.

The forward visibility in cruise is less than panoramic. *Ray Conkling*

Left
Pete Miller designed the airframe for 12g at 450mph. This provides adequate margins for high speeds and rough air. *Ray Conkling*

Granvilles showed up everywhere.
From the left: Steve Wolf, Delmar Benjamin, Debbie Trewheela (Mark Granville's daughter), June Dakin and Paul Granville (Tom Granville's daughter and son), Pete Miller, Tim Jones (Gladys Granville and Hiram Jones' grandson), Barbara Granville (Tom Granville's daughter), Tom Jones (Gladys Granville and Hiram Jones's son). *EAA*

Right
Plenty of time is available to reflect on the past during the long cross-country trips. Looking down on the landscape one can almost visualize the country as it would have appeared to Lee Gehlbach back in 1932. *Ray Conkling*

Granville Brothers Aircraft Lineage

Gee Bee Model A
Number Built: 9
Type: 2-place biplane for private use
Engine: Kinner-12-5, 118hp
Granted government group 2 approval (2-194), March 18, 1930

Gee Bee Sportsters
Type: single seat, low wing private plane
Number Built: 8

Registration #	Engine	Pilot
NR-49V	Cirrus 110	Bayles
NR-845Y	Cirrus 110	Moon
NC-855Y	Menasco C-4 125hp	Rand
NC-856Y	Warner Scarab 110hp	Nott
NC-46Y	Warner Scarab 110hp	Unknown
NC-72V	Warner Scarab 110hp	Sloan
NC-11043	Menasco-C4 125hp	Granville
NC-1044	Warner Scarab 110hp	Harris, Tibert

Gee Bee Senior Sportsters
Type: 2-place for private use, stressed for aerobatics
Number Built: 2

Registration #	Engine	Pilot
X-11049	Wasp C	Maude Tait
X-715Y	Lycoming	Cord Corporation

Gee Bee Super Sportsters
Type: racers built for world speed attempts, closed course races, and timed runs
Number Built : 3

Model	Engine	Pilot
Model Z	Wasp Jr.	Robert Hall
		Lowell Bayles
Model R-1	Wasp Senior T3d1, 550hp (700hp race)	Russell Boardman
		Jimmy Doolittle
Model R-2	Wasp Jr., 530hp	Russell Boardman
		Russell Thaw
		Lee Gehlbach
		Jimmy Haizlip

Gee Bee Long-Tail Racer
Type: Racer built from R-1 and R-2 wreckage (R-1 fuselage and R-2 wings), 1.5ft longer
Number Built: 1

Model	Engine	Pilot
Model R1/R2	Hornet	Roy Minor
		Cecil Allen

Granville Brothers Aircraft, Inc., liquidated in the fall of 1933. They built a total of twenty-two airplanes. This included nine biplanes, eight sportsters, two senior sportsters, three super sportsters, and one long-tail racer. They had a large, cantilever monoplane under construction that disappeared into history. After liquidation, the workforce went on to build the *QED* for the 1934 England-to-Australia race and *Time Flies*, a racer for Frank Hawks.

Benjamin at the prop of Jim Jenkins' Gee Bee Model E replica. *Premo Galletti*